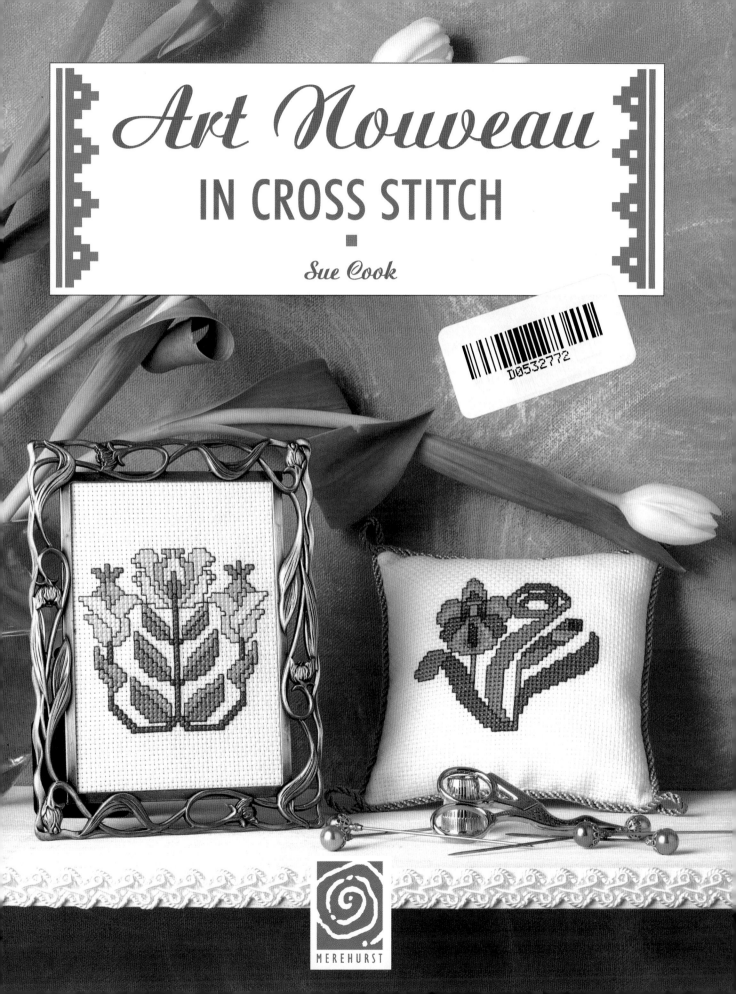

Art Nouveau

IN CROSS STITCH

■

Sue Cook

MEREHURST

THE CHARTS

Some of the designs in this book are very detailed and, due to
inevitable space limitations, the charts may be shown on a
comparatively small scale; in such cases, readers may find it helpful
to have the particular chart with which they are currently
working enlarged.

THREADS

The projects in this book were all stitched with DMC stranded
cotton embroidery threads. The keys given with each chart also list
thread combinations for those who wish to use Anchor or Madeira
embroidery threads. It should be pointed out that the shades produced
by different companies vary slightly, and it is not always possible to
find identical colours in a different range.

Published in 1999 by Merehurst Limited
Ferry House, 51-57 Lacy Road, Putney, London SW15 1PR
Copyright © 1999 Merehurst Limited
ISBN 1 85391 759 1

A catalogue record for this book is available from the British Library.

Editor: Heather Dewhurst
Designer: Maggie Aldred
Photographer: Juliet Piddington
Illustrators: King & King Design Associates and John Hutchinson
Senior Commissioning Editor: Karen Hemingway
CEO and Publisher: Anne Wilson
International Sales Director: Mark Newman
Colour separation by Bright Arts (HK) Ltd
Printed in Hong Kong by Wing King Tong

*Merehurst is the leading publisher of craft books and has an excellent
range of titles to suit all levels. Please send to the address above for our
free catalogue, stating the title of this book.*

CONTENTS

INTRODUCTION

The vogue for Art Nouveau reached its peak towards the end of the last century. Artists and designers used its graceful, flowing lines to adorn everything from jewellery to buildings. Now, at the turn of another century, the designs still have a magic. I have always had a fascination for this style and was delighted to have a chance to produce designs for this book. It was a real challenge to interpret the sinuous shapes, many based on nature, into the grid of cross stitch. Using styles based on work of many of the most famous designers of Art Nouveau, I have tried to produce designs for all abilities.

There are four graceful floral projects which use only whole stitches and which can be stitched quickly to make a beautiful gift or card. The more formal style of topiary trees and stylized flowers make them perfect designs for desktop items. Fans of Charles Rennie Mackintosh will find a sampler based on his 'Glasgow Rose' full of motifs suitable for other projects. An elegant peacock fits perfectly in the lid of a needlework box and nasturtium borders in a choice of colours entwine across table linen. Experienced stitchers will relish the challenge of producing a Mucha-style beauty, whose flowing hair is dressed with honeysuckle and ornaments.

A cushion with a centre panel based on the glowing colours of Tiffany glass makes a luxurious project for a bedroom. Or you could stitch some little treasures based on Tiffany's most famous designs to make special gifts. Whatever you choose, I hope you enjoy producing your very own piece of Art Nouveau.

BASIC SKILLS

BEFORE YOU BEGIN

PREPARING THE FABRIC
Even with an average amount of handling, many evenweave fabrics tend to fray at the edges, so it is a good idea to overcast the raw edges, using ordinary sewing thread, before you begin.

FABRIC
The projects in this book are stitched on both Aida and evenweave fabric. Aida fabric is manufactured so that the threads appear as 'blocks' - one block equalling one stitch. Counting is easy, making this a good choice for beginners. The fabric 'count' refers to the number of stitches per inch (2.5cm); the higher the number the smaller the finished design will be.

Evenweave fabric is woven with an equal number of vertical and horizontal threads. Cross stitch is normally worked over two threads (vertically and horizontally) on these fabrics, giving designs worked on 28-count the same finished size as 14-count Aida.

Most of the projects in this book are interchangeable between Aida fabric and evenweave fabric, with the possible exception of 'Honeysuckle Beauty' where the large number of fractional stitches makes Aida impractical. Several designs have been sewn on to black fabric. For ease of working, stitch as much as possible in natural light or place something white across your lap to make the holes easier to see.

THE INSTRUCTIONS
Each project begins with a full list of the materials that you will require to complete the project successfully. The measurements given for the embroidery fabric include a minimum of 5cm (2in) all around to allow for preparing the edges to prevent them from fraying.

Colour keys for stranded embroidery cottons — DMC, Anchor or Madeira — are given with each chart. It is assumed that you will need to buy one skein of each colour mentioned in a particular key, even though you may use less.

Where metallic threads have been used, the specific make of thread is listed, without giving any equivalent. Several manufacturers produce these threads, but each brand will vary significantly, and it is not always possible to find a close equivalent. If you are unable to obtain the named thread, you may be able to substitute a similar thread for an equally attractive, if perhaps slightly different, effect, but you should experiment to ensure that you achieve a good coverage of the fabric before using it in your finished embroidery.

Before you begin to embroider, always mark the centre of the design with two lines of basting stitches, one vertical and one horizontal, running from edge to edge of the fabric (to find the centre on the chart, count the maximum number of stitches each way and divide by two).

As you stitch, use the centre lines given on the chart and the basting threads on your fabric as reference points for counting the squares and threads to position your design accurately.

WORKING IN A HOOP

A hoop is the most popular frame for use with small areas of embroidery. It consists of two rings, one fitted inside the other; the outer ring usually has an adjustable screw attachment so that it can be tightened to hold the stretched fabric in place. Hoops are available in several sizes, ranging from 10cm (4in) in diameter to quilting hoops with a diameter of 38cm (15in). Hoops with table stands or floor stands attached are also available.

1 To stretch your fabric in a hoop, place the area to be embroidered over the inner ring and press the outer ring over it, with the tension screw released. Tissue paper can be placed between the outer ring and the embroidery, so that the hoop does not mark the fabric. Lay the tissue paper over the fabric when

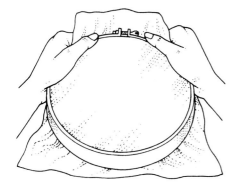

you set it in the hoop, then tear away the central embroidery area.

2 Smooth the fabric and straighten the grain before tightening. The fabric should be evenly stretched.

WORKING IN A RECTANGULAR FRAME

Rectangular frames are more suitable for larger pieces of embroidery. They consist of two rollers, with tapes attached, and two flat side pieces, which slot into the rollers and are held in place by pegs or screw attachments. Available in different sizes, either alone or with adjustable table or floor stands, frames are measured by the length of the roller tape, and range in size from 30cm (12in) to 68cm (27in). As alternatives to a slate frame, canvas stretchers and the backs of old picture frames can be used. Provided there is sufficient extra fabric around the finished size of the embroidery, the edges can be turned under and simply attached with drawing pins (thumb tacks) or staples.

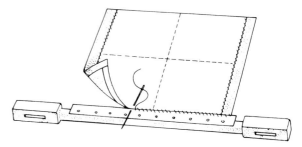

1 To stretch your fabric in a rectangular frame, cut out the fabric, allowing at least an extra 5cm (2in) all around the finished size of the embroidery. Baste a single 12mm (½in) turning on the top and bottom edges and oversew strong tape, 2.5cm (1in) wide, to the other two sides. Mark the centre line both ways with basting stitches. Working from the centre outwards and using strong thread, oversew the top and bottom edges to the roller tapes. Fit the side

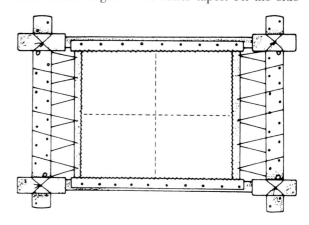

pieces into the slots and roll any extra fabric on one roller until the fabric is taut.

2 Insert the pegs or adjust the screw attachments to secure the frame. Thread a large-eyed needle (chenille needle) with strong thread or fine string and lace both edges, securing the ends around the intersections of the frame. Lace the webbing at 2.5cm (1in) intervals, stretching the fabric evenly.

THE STITCHES

CROSS STITCH

For all cross stitch embroidery, the following two methods of working are used. In each case, neat rows of vertical stitches are produced on the back of the fabric.

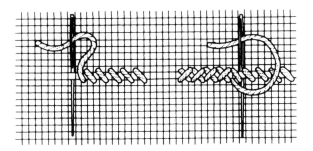

• When stitching large areas, work in horizontal rows. Working from right to left, complete the first row of evenly spaced diagonal stitches over the number of threads specified in the project instructions. Then, working from left to right, repeat the process. Continue in this way, making sure each stitch crosses in the same direction.

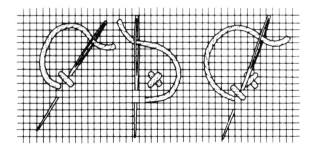

• When stitching diagonal lines, work downwards, completing each stitch before moving to the next. When starting a project, always begin to embroider at the centre of the design and work outwards to ensure that the design will be placed centrally on the fabric.

BACKSTITCH

Backstitch is used in the projects to give emphasis to a particular foldline, an outline or a shadow. The stitches are worked over the same number of threads as the cross stitch, forming continuous straight or diagonal lines.

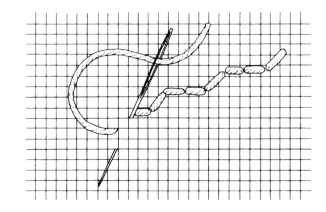

• Make the first stitch from left to right; pass the needle behind the fabric and bring it out one stitch length ahead to the left. Repeat and continue in this way along the line.

To give a rounded effect on curves in some designs, backstitch is laid over two squares to give a 'long-line' and is usually placed over a three-quarter stitch which fills the largest portion of the fabric to be outlined.

THREE-QUARTER CROSS STITCH

Some fractional stitches are used on certain projects in this book; although they strike fear into the hearts of less experienced stitchers they are not difficult to master, and give a more natural line in certain instances. Should you find it difficult to pierce the centre of the Aida block, simply use a sharp needle to make a small hole in the centre first.

To work a three-quarter cross, bring the needle up at point A and down through the centre of the square at B. Later, a diagonal backstitch finishes the stitch. A chart square with two different symbols

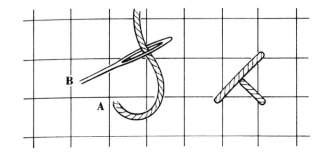

separated by a diagonal line requires two 'three-quarter' stitches. Backstitch will finish the square.

ATTACHING BEADS

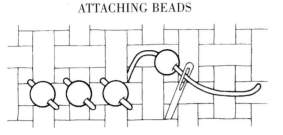

Some projects in this book use beads to add interest. These are either represented by a symbol on the chart or full description of the beads will be listed in the instructions. Beading needles are available but are often very fine and difficult to handle. A No.26 tapestry needle will pass through the eye of most seed beads and they are normally attached when the rest of the stitching is complete. Stitch on using a half cross stitch from upper left to lower right, finishing off securely.

SPECIALIST THREADS

Both silky blending filaments and metallic braids are used in some of these projects. Some require the blending filament to be blended with stranded cotton while in others it is used singly. In each case, clear instructions are given in the text as to how many threads of each to use. For ease of working with blending filament, slightly dampen the thread before knotting it into the needle and then threading on the stranded cotton (not suitable for metallic threads). Metallic braids and blending filament should only be used in short lengths to prevent tangling and to stop the fibres 'stripping' off as the thread is pulled through the fabric.

To thread blending filament, double the thread about 5cm (2in) at one end, and insert the loop through the eye of the needle. Pull the loop over the point of the needle and gently pull the loop towards the end of the eye to secure the thread to the needle. If you are using a combination of blending filament and stranded cotton, thread the latter through the eye in the usual way, and clip it to match the length of the blending filament.

MOUNTING EMBROIDERY

The cardboard should be cut to the size of the finished embroidery, with an extra amount added all round to allow for the recess in the frame.

LIGHTWEIGHT FABRICS

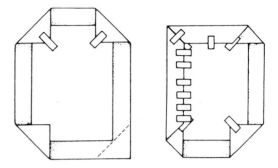

1 Place the embroidery face down, with the cardboard centred on top, and basting and pencil lines matching. Begin by folding over the fabric at each corner and securing it with masking tape.

2 Working first on one side and then the other, fold over the fabric on all sides and secure it firmly with pieces of masking tape which are placed about 2.5cm (1in) apart. Also neaten the mitred corners with masking tape, pulling the fabric tightly to give a firm, smooth finish.

HEAVIER FABRICS

Lay the embroidery face down, with the cardboard centred on top; fold over the edges of the fabric on opposite sides, making mitred folds at the corners, and lace across, using strong thread. Repeat on the other two sides. Finally, pull up the fabric firmly over the cardboard. Overstitch the mitred corners.

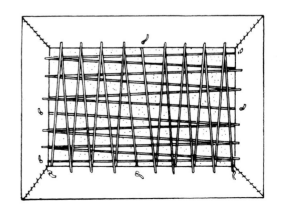

Honeysuckle Beauty

Alphonse Mucha created some of the most stunning Art Nouveau images, many of which are still popular today. Adorned with jewels and flowers, this beautiful design is typical of his decadent style and a challenge to experienced stitchers.

HONEYSUCKLE BEAUTY

YOU WILL NEED

For the Picture, with a design area measuring
19cm x 17.5cm (7½in x 7in):

*35cm (14in) square of pale peach, 28-count
evenweave fabric*
*Stranded embroidery cotton and specialist thread in
the colours listed in the panel*
No.26 tapestry needle
Brass charm for hair ornament (optional)
Seed beads in the colours listed in the panel
Firm card for backing
Strong thread for lacing
Frame and mount of your choice

•

THE EMBROIDERY

Prepare the fabric and find the centre point as explained on page 4. Using two strands of thread in the needle (unless indicated in the key), work the cross stitching over two threads of fabric. When stitching with rayon blending filament or metallic braid, refer to the instructions on page 7.

I have used a piece from an old necklace to make part of the hair ornament but a suitable brass charm would work just as well. The ornament is suspended from a gold chain which can be completed in chain stitch or backstitch.

Work the backstitch using one strand of thead, as listed in the key. Then, using one strand of Kreinik gold braid No.8 (017HL), form the gold fringing on the scarf with straight stitches. Add deep blue beads at the end of each stitch (see page 7).

Using one strand of gold braid as above, outline the enamelled hair ornament (on the left). Using two strands of dark green, stitch the stems of honeysuckle seed heads. Complete the end of each spike in old gold beads.

FINISHING

Remove the finished embroidery from the frame and press lightly on the wrong side (avoid using steam which can affect metallic thread). Mount and frame your picture following the instructions given on page 7. Alternatively, take your project to a professional framer.

▶ HONEYSUCKLE BEAUTY	DMC	ANCHOR	MADEIRA	MARLITT/ KREINIK
— White	01	02	2402	-
↓ Gold braid				Kreinik No.8 017HL
⌐ Light purple x 1 plus medium purple x 1	210	108	0802	857
♥ Black	310	403	2400	-
● Medium brown	434	310	2009	-
:: Light brown	436	1045	2011	-
⌟ Purple x 1 plus medium purple rayon x 1	550	99	0713	858
⌐ Dark purple x 1 plus medium purple rayon x 1	552	101	0714	858
⌐ Medium purple x 1 plus light purple rayon x 1	554	96	0711	857
·• Medium blue	597	168	1110	-
× Medium blue x 1 plus medium blue rayon x 1	597	168	1110	1053
♡ Blue	598	167	1111	-
R Reddish brown	632	936	2311	-
▽ Dark gold	680	901	2210	-
∕ Ecru	712	926	2101	-
＼ Tangerine	742	303	0114	-
∧ Yellow	744	301	0112	-
+ Pale yellow	745	300	0111	-
⁜ Peach	758	9575	2309	-
⊹ Plum x 1	778	968	0808	-
T Brown	801	359	2007	-
— Olive	831	277	2201	-
O Light olive	833	907	2203	-
Dark brown*	838	380	2005	-
■ Dark plum x 1 plus cerise rayon x 1	915	1029	0705	863
⋊ Medium peach	945	881	2313	-
• Light peach	951	1010	2308	-
∕′ Light pink	963	73	0503	-
→ Turquoise	964	185	1112	-
↑ Medium aqua	993	186	1201	-
•• Dark peach	3064	260	2312	-
▼ Dark green	3345	268	1406	-
⊒ Green	3347	266	1408	-
S Medium pink	3354	74	2610	-
▲ Dark pink x 1 plus cerise rayon x 1	3607	87	0708	863
I Pink x 1 plus light purple rayon x 1	3609	85	0710	1214
Ⱪ Dark cerise	3721	896	0811	-
H Cerise	3731	76	0506	-
Y Light cerise	3733	75	0504	-
⋌ Light plum x 1	3743	869	2611	-
◇ Light flesh	3770	1009	2314	-
← Coral	3778	1013	2312	-
Ⱪ Dark aqua	3809	169	2507	-
L Light aqua	3811	928	1002	-
N Aqua	3814	187	1203	-
⭦ Gold x 1 plus gold blending filament x 1	3820	306	2509	Kreinik Gold 002
▣ Light gold x 1 plus gold blending filament x 1	3822	295	0112	Kreinik Gold 002
Ⅎ Cream x 1 plus gold blending filament x 1	3823	386	2511	Kreinik Gold 002
T Cream	3823	386	2511	-
Deep blue beads	V3.04.930			
Old gold beads	V3.12.823			

Note: Backstitch end of nose, upper lip and lips in peach; upper and lower eyelids in medium brown; outer edge of gold 'frame' in dark gold; remainder of outlining in dark brown*. Form nostrils with two small straight stitches in dark brown* (*used for backstitch and straight stitch only).

Elegant Florals

These simple designs use only whole stitches, making them quick to sew. The flowing lines of the iris and poppy are complemented by the linear style of the lily and begonia. Look for special trimmings or frames to show off your projects.

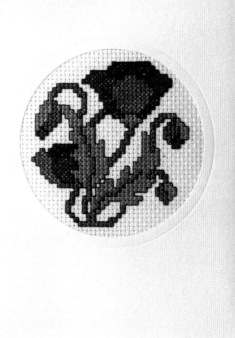

ELEGANT FLORALS

YOU WILL NEED

For the Poppy Card, with a design area measuring 7cm (2³⁄₄in) square:

15cm (6in) square of cream, 14-count Aida fabric
Stranded embroidery cotton in the colours
listed in the appropriate panel
No.26 tapestry needle
Cream greetings card with circular aperture
measuring 7.5cm (3in) in diameter
Doubled-sided tape

For the Iris Pincushion, with a design area measuring 8.5cm x 8cm (3³⁄₄in x 3¹⁄₄in):

15cm (6in) square of cream, 14-count Aida fabric
Stranded embroidery cotton in the colours
listed in the appropriate panel
No.26 tapestry needle
15cm (6in) square of cream fabric for backing
Pins
Matching sewing thread
Polyester filling
1m (40in) of contrasting narrow silk cord

For the Lily Picture, with a design area measuring 8cm x 7.5cm (3¹⁄₄in x 3in):

20cm (8in) square of cream, 14-count Aida fabric
Stranded embroidery cotton in the colours
listed in the appropriate panel
No.26 tapestry needle
Frame of your choice

For the Begonia Appliqué, with a design area measuring 8cm (3¹⁄₄in) square:

Zweigart pre-made appliqué 5532/17 in grey
measuring 67 x 53 stitches (see page 40)
Stranded embroidery cotton in the colours
listed in the appropriate panel
No.26 tapestry needle
15cm (6in) square of stiff white card
Double-sided tape
20cm (8in) square of white self-adhesive felt
10cm (4in) of ribbon, 3mm (¹⁄₈in) wide
Clear glue

THE EMBROIDERY

For each of the designs shown, prepare your fabric and find the centre as explained on page 4. Using two strands of thread, complete all the cross stitching. Then, with one strand of thread, complete all the backstitching. Remove the embroidery from the frame and wash, then press on the wrong side.

THE GREETINGS CARD

Trim the embroidery to 12mm (¹⁄₂in) larger all round than the card aperture. Place double-sided tape around the opening and press the design into place. Fold the card and secure with double-sided tape for a neat finish.

THE FRAMED PICTURE

Trim the embroidery to 2.5cm (1in) larger than the board provided with the frame. Follow the instructions on page 7 to lace the embroidery to the board, then assemble the frame.

THE PINCUSHION

Pin the embroidery to the cream fabric, right sides together. Leaving a 12mm (¹⁄₂in) seam allowance, stitch around the edges, leaving an opening. Turn the pincushion the right side out, stuff with polyester filling, then slipstitch the opening closed. Slipstitch silk cord around the edges of the pincushion, making a loop at each corner.

THE APPLIQUÉ

To make the appliqué into a picture, stick an oval of white card to the wrong side of the stitched piece and press down firmly. Peel the backing from the self-adhesive felt and lay the appliqué, wrong side down, on the sticky surface and press firmly. Following the edge of the appliqué, trim the felt to size. Finally, fold the ribbon in half and attach it to the back with glue to form a hanging loop.

▶ LILY		DMC	ANCHOR	MADEI
▬	Orange	740	316	0202
◇	Light orange	742	303	0201
↑	Yellow	744	301	0112
	Dark brown*	838	380	2005
▲	Dark olive	3011	845	1607
✠	Medium olive	3012	844	1606
♡	Light olive	3013	842	1605
╱	Cream	3823	386	2511

Note: Backstitch outlines with dark brown* (*used for backstitch only).

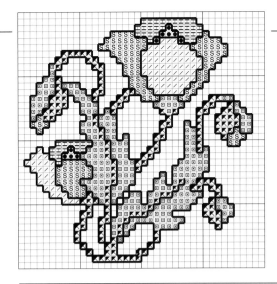

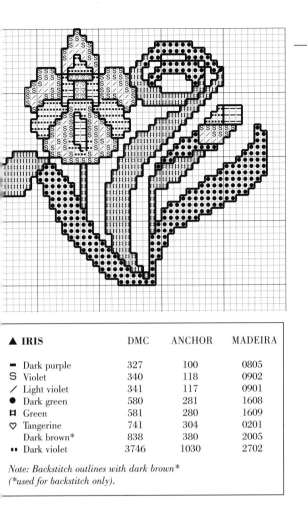

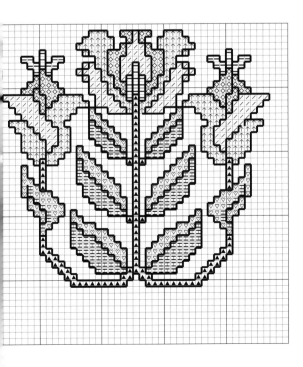

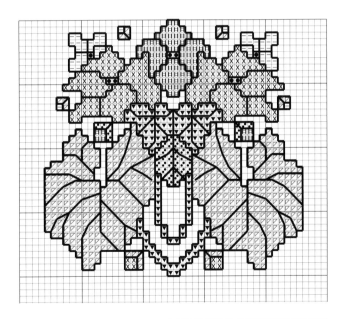

▲ IRIS	DMC	ANCHOR	MADEIRA
▬ Dark purple	327	100	0805
S Violet	340	118	0902
⁄ Light violet	341	117	0901
● Dark green	580	281	1608
⊞ Green	581	280	1609
♡ Tangerine	741	304	0201
Dark brown*	838	380	2005
▪▪ Dark violet	3746	1030	2702

Note: Backstitch outlines with dark brown*
(*used for backstitch only).

▲ POPPY	DMC	ANCHOR	MADEIRA
⁄ Light red	350	11	0213
⊏ Dark red	814	45	0514
S Red	817	13	0211
● Dark brown	838	380	2005
⋉ Dark green	3051	681	1508
⊡ Green	3052	859	1509

Note: Backstitch outlines with dark brown.

▲ BEGONIA	DMC	ANCHOR	MADEIRA
● Dark brown	838	380	2005
▼ Dark olive	3011	845	1607
▽ Medium olive	3012	844	1606
·⁖ Light olive	3013	842	1605
⊞ Dark pink	3705	35	0410
✕ Medium pink	3706	33	0409
▬ Light pink	3708	31	0408

Note: Backstitch outlines with dark brown.

Tiffany Iris Cushion

Louis Comfort Tiffany used the wealth of his family jewellery firm to pioneer new methods of producing glass. Famous for his lamps, many patrons commissioned him to design windows. Here, the black fabric sets off the glowing colours of his iris.

TIFFANY IRIS CUSHION

YOU WILL NEED

For the Cushion, with a design area measuring
17.5cm x 16cm (7in x 6³/₈in):

*33cm (13in) square of black, 28-count
evenweave fabric*
*Stranded embroidery cotton in the colours
listed in the panel*
No.26 tapestry needle
33cm (13in) square of black fabric for backing
Pins
Matching sewing thread
30cm (12in) cushion pad or polyester filling
1.5m of black silk cord, 6mm (¹/₄in) wide
4 black silk tassels

●

THE EMBROIDERY

Prepare the fabric and find the centre point as
explained on page 4. Using two strands of thread in
the needle and stitching over two threads of the
fabric, complete all the cross stitching following the
chart. Work the backstitch using two strands of
thread in the needle.

FINISHING

Remove the completed embroidery from the frame
and press lightly on the wrong side. Place the
stitched piece on to the backing fabric with right
sides together, and pin. Leaving a 12mm (¹/₂in)
seam allowance, stitch around the edges, leaving an
opening on the lower edge for turning. Snip the corners, turn the cushion cover the right side out, and
press. Insert a cushion pad or polyester filling, then
slipstitch the opening closed. Slipstitch the cord to
the outer edges of the cushion cover, and stitch a
tassel to each corner to finish.

▶ TIFFANY IRIS	DMC	ANCHOR	MADEIRA
● White	01	02	2402
Black*	310	403	Black
♥ Plum	316	1017	0809
▽ Dark purple	327	100	0805
T Dark blue	333	119	0903
◇ Violet	340	118	0902
+ Light violet	341	117	0901
▬ Dark green	469	268	1503
▪▪ Medium green	470	267	1502
O Green	471	266	1501
− Light green	472	253	1414
⟍ Medium purple	553	98	0712
ꓘ Dark gold	680	901	2210
∷ Dark olive	730	845	1614
ꭍ Medium olive	732	281	1612
S Light olive	733	280	1611
▽ Tangerine	742	303	0114
← Yellow	744	301	0112
⟋ Cream	746	275	2511
ꟼ Light plum	778	968	0808
Ɜ Aqua	806	168	2506
∕ Light pink	818	23	0502
● Dark grey	844	1041	1810
Ⴌ Dark violet	3746	1030	2702
Y Light blue	3747	120	1001
⊥ Light aqua	3766	167	1105
I Light yellow	3823	386	2511

*Note: Backstitch 'leading' on inner and outer edges, and dividers
in border, with black* (*used for backstitch only).*

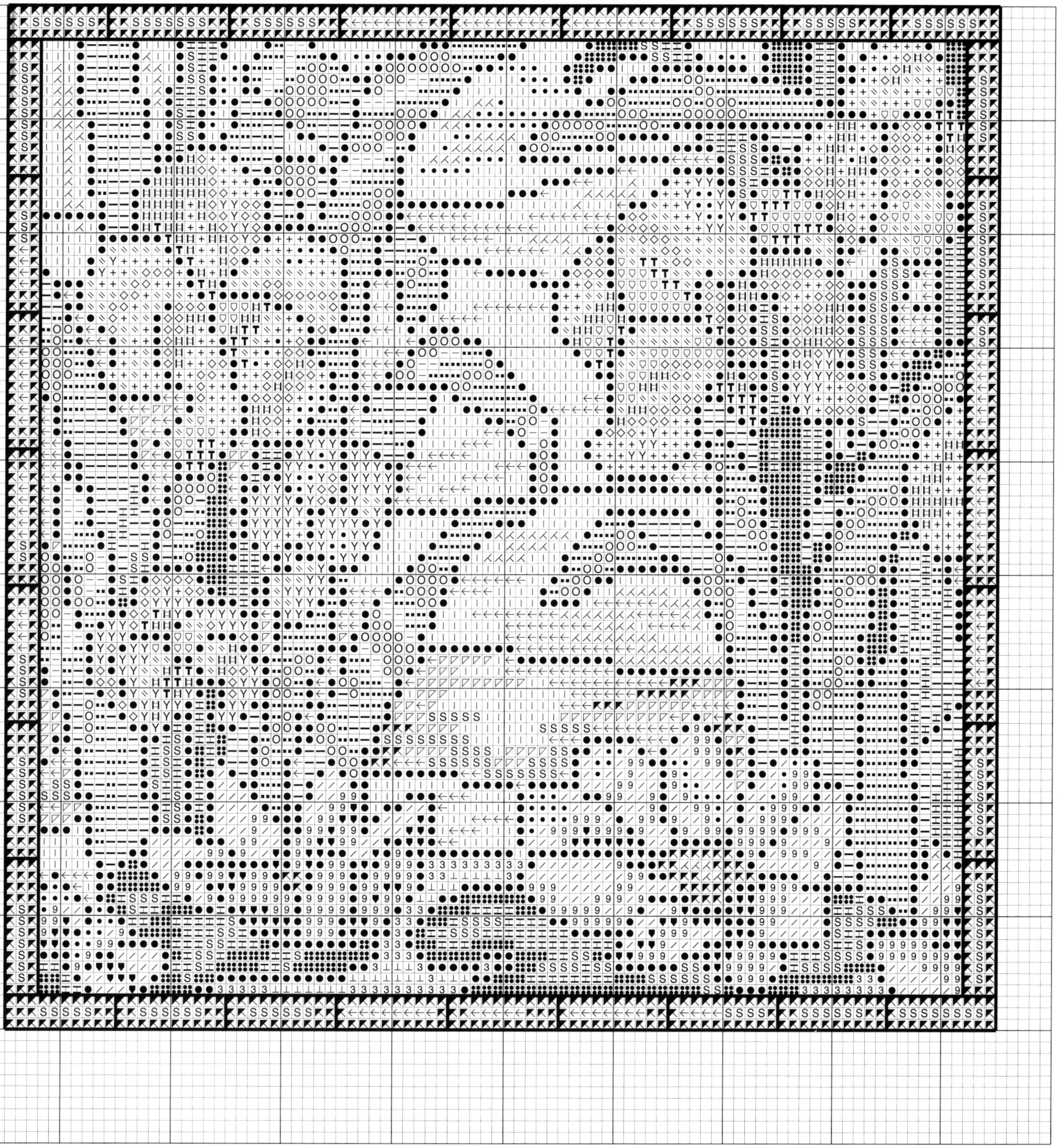

Tiffany Treasures

Stitch a tiny treasure for a special friend. The dragonfly, based on a stained glass suncatcher, fits on to a spectacles case. A fragment of Tiffany's 'Dogwood' design adorns a powder compact and a miniature lamp decorates a trinket box lid.

TIFFANY TREASURES

YOU WILL NEED

For the Spectacles Case, with a design area
measuring 7.5cm x 5cm (3in x 2in):

*Ready-made black quilted spectacles case
with 18-count Aida fabric insert
(for suppliers, see page 40)
Stranded embroidery cotton and specialist thread in
the colours listed in the appropriate panel
No.26 tapestry needle*

For the Powder Compact, with a design area
measuring 6.5cm (2¹/₂in) in diameter:

*15cm (6in) square of black, 28-count
evenweave fabric
Stranded embroidery cotton in the colours
listed in the appropriate panel
No.26 tapestry needle
Powder compact (for suppliers, see page 40)*

For the Trinket box, with a design area measuring
7.5cm x 5cm (3in x 2in):

*15cm (6in) square of black, 28-count
evenweave fabric
Stranded embroidery cotton and specialist thread in
the colours listed in the appropriate panel
No.26 tapestry needle
Trinket box (for suppliers, see page 40)*

●

THE SPECTACLES CASE

Find the centre of Aida fabric flap on the case (the
most accurate way to do this is count the number of
squares in each direction). Refer to the instructions
on page 7 for working with specialist threads. Using
one strand of stranded cotton or rayon thread, complete all the cross stitching following the chart.
Work the backstitch using two strands of thread in
the needle. Lightly press the flap on the wrong side.

THE POWDER COMPACT

Prepare the fabric and find the centre point as
explained on page 4. Using two strands of thread in
the needle and stitching over two threads of fabric,
complete all the cross stitching following the chart.
Work the backstitching using one strand of thread
in the needle. Assemble the compact according to
the manufacturer's instructions. (Note that the
design will go right to the edges of the compact lid
with no fabric showing.)

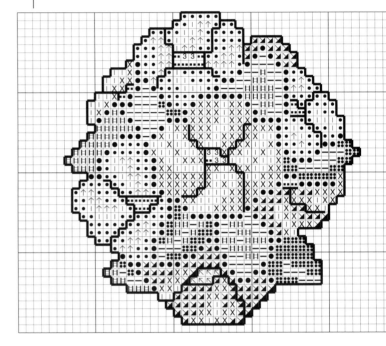

▲ DOGWOOD COMPACT		DMC	ANCHOR	MADEIRA
•	White	01	02	2402
▬	Green	470	268	1503
⊞	Medium green	471	266	1501
3	Yellow	727	293	0110
↖	Tangerine	742	303	0114
◼◼	Gold	783	307	2211
⏐	Light pink	818	230	502
	Dark brown*	838	380	2005
●	Dark grey	844	1041	1810
∷	Dark green	937	269	1504
◢	Dark pink	961	76	0610
✕	Medium pink	962	75	0609
↑	Cream	3823	386	2511

Note: Backstitch outlines using dark brown (*used for backstitch only).*

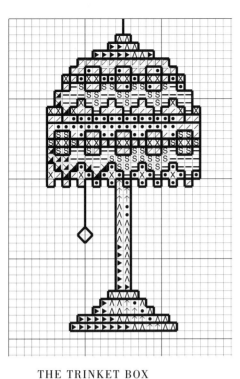

◄ LAMP TRINKET BOX	DMC	ANCHOR	MADEIRA	MARLITT/ KREINIK
Black*	310	403	Black	-
⬊ Dark purple x 2 plus purple rayon x 1	550	101	0714	819
▬ Purple x 2 plus medium purple rayon x 1	552	99	0713	858
• White	01	02	2402	-
▽ Light purple	211	342	0801	-
S Medium purple	554	96	0711	-
∧ Yellow	725	305	0108	-
↑ Light yellow	727	293	0110	-
✕ Tangerine	742	303	0114	-
► Gold	783	307	2211	-
╱ Cream	3823	386	2511	-
Bright yellow*	-	-	-	Kreinik No.8 Braid 091

Note: Backstitch switch cord and metal spike on top of lamp with Kreinik Bright Yellow; backstitch the rest of the outlines in one strand of black* (*used for backstitch only).*

THE TRINKET BOX

Prepare the fabric and find the centre point as explained on page 4. Some areas of the design require stranded cotton and rayon blending filament to be blended. Using two strands of cotton and one of rayon, follow the instructions on page 7 for working with specialist threads. Complete the back-stitch details, following the key. Assemble the box lid according to the manufacturer's instructions.

▼ DRAGONFLY CASE	DMC	ANCHOR	MADEIRA	MARLITT
• White	01	02	2402	-
Black*	310	403	Black	-
● Orange	608	332	0205	-
← Tangerine	742	303	0114	-
◇ Yellow	744	301	0112	-
◤ Aqua	-	-	-	1053
∷ Dark aqua	-	-	-	1056
✕ Light blue	3811	928	1111	-
Ɩ Cream	3823	386	2511	-

Note: Backstitch outlines using two strands of black (*used for backstitch only).*

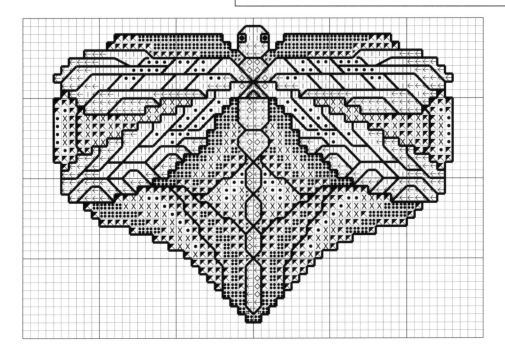

Nasturtium Table Linen

These entwined borders were adapted from a style book entitled *La Plante*, which was published at the turn of the century. Perfect for table linen, you can stitch these borders in bright natural colours or subtle toning shades for a sophisticated look.

NASTURTIUM
TABLE LINEN

YOU WILL NEED

For each Table Mat, measuring
30cm (12in) square:

*33cm (13in) square of antique cream, 28-count
evenweave fabric
Stranded embroidery cotton in the colours
listed in the appropriate panel
No.26 tapestry needle
30cm (12in) square of white or cream
cotton for backing
Matching sewing thread*

•

THE EMBROIDERY

Prepare the fabric and find the centre referring to
the instructions on page 4; this will help with the
placement of the borders. Decide how far from the
edge of the fabric you wish to start your border,
allowing for a hem of approximately 12mm (^{1}/2in).
You may wish to run a line of light basting stitches
to indicate the start and finish of your border. Use
the pattern repeat to decide how many repeats will
comfortably fit on your fabric. When ready to stitch,
start from the centre of the pattern repeat. Using two
strands of thread in the needle and stitching over
two threads of the fabric, complete all the cross
stitching following the chart. Work the backstitching using one strand of thread in the needle.

To stitch the horizontal border in the toning
colourway, replace dark and medium green in
leaves with brown; medium green in stems and
buds with dark brown; dark orange with medium
brown; and light orange with light brown.

To stitch the vertical border in the bright colourway, replace light brown with light orange; dark
brown with dark green; brown with medium green;
and medium brown with dark orange.

Note that the bright colourway has five shades
and the toning colourway only four. The centre of
the flowers are stitched in dark brown in both
options.

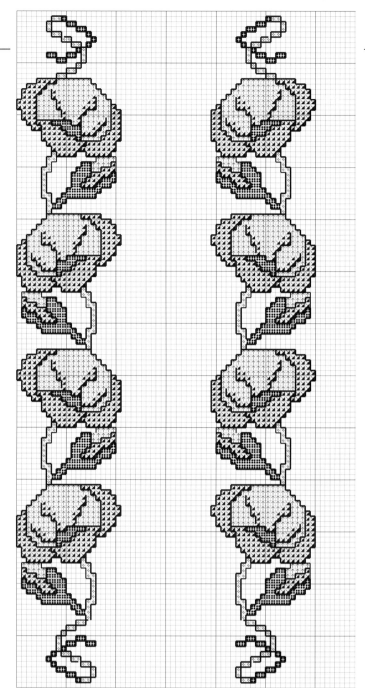

▶▲ VERTICAL NASTURTIUMS	DMC	ANCHOR	MADEIRA
Toning colourway			
↘ Brown	400	351	2305
↑ Light brown	402	1047	2307
∷ Dark brown	938	381	2005
↘ Medium brown	3776	1048	1105
Bright colourway			
↘ Medium green	471	266	1501
↑ Light orange	741	304	0201
∷ Dark green	469	267	1503
↘ Dark orange	608	332	0205
▼ Dark brown	938	381	2005

Note: Backstitch outlines in dark brown.

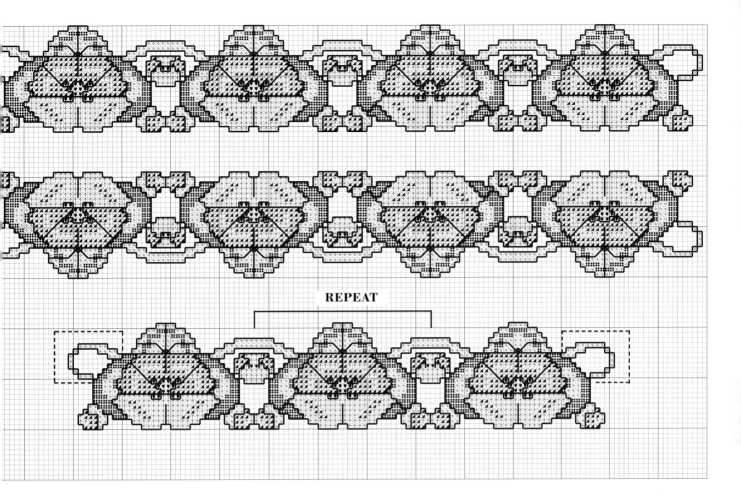

REPEAT

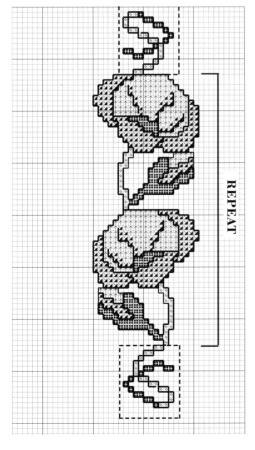

REPEAT

▲ HORIZONTAL NASTURTIUMS	DMC	ANCHOR	MADEIRA
Bright colourway			
∷ Dark green	469	267	1503
↘ Medium green	471	266	1501
◣ Dark orange	608	332	0205
↑ Light orange	741	304	0201
♥ Dark brown	938	381	2005
Toning colourway			
↘ Brown	400	351	2305
∷ Dark brown	938	381	2005
◣ Medium brown	3776	1048	1105
↑ Light brown	402	1047	2307

Note: Backstitch outlines in dark brown.

FINISHING

Remove the embroidery from the frame. Turn and press a 12mm (1/2in) hem all around the stitched piece. With wrong sides together, place the stitched piece on to the backing fabric. Turn the hem edges on to the backing, slipstitch into place, and press.

Glasgow Roses

Charles Rennie Mackintosh was one of the most influential architects of his day. Together with his wife Margaret, he created restful interiors and the rose was one of their favourite symbols. Stitch a sampler or smaller items in this style.

GLASGOW ROSES

YOU WILL NEED

For the Sampler, with a design area measuring
18.5cm x 16.5cm (7³⁄₈in x 6¹⁄₂in):

30cm x 35cm (12in x 14in) of antique white,
28-count evenweave fabric
Stranded embroidery cotton in the colours
listed in the panel
No.26 tapestry needle
Firm card for backing
Frame and mount of your choice

For other Projects:

Antique white 18-count Aida, in size required
Stranded embroidery cotton in the colours
listed in the panel
No.26 tapestry needle
Door finger plate (for suppliers, see page 40)
Trinket box (for suppliers, see page 40)
Mirror and hairbrush set (for suppliers,
see page 40)

●

THE EMBROIDERY

Prepare the fabric and find the centre point as explained on page 4. Using two strands of thread in the needle and stitching over two threads of the fabric, complete all the cross stitching following the chart. Then work the backstitching using one strand of thread in the needle.

FINISHING

Remove the embroidery from the frame and wash, if necessary, then press lightly on the wrong side. An excellent choice of ready-made frames and mounts is now widely available from art and craft stores. If you wish to carry out your own framing, follow the instructions given on page 7 for lacing the stitched piece securely on to the cardboard. Alternatively, take your sampler to a professional framer who will advise you on suitable mounts and frame finishes.

MAKING OTHER PROJECTS

Glasgow Roses is a versatile design which allows you to create your own unique projects. Here, elements from the sampler have been made into inserts for a door finger plate, a silver trinket box and a beautiful mirror and hairbrush.

To extract elements from the design, make an enlarged photocopy of the design. If you are stitching a piece to insert in a ready-made item it is important to have an exact measurement of the actual design space available. Choose part of the design, for example, the large central rose and count the number of stitches widthways and lengthways. Divide each of these measurements by two and this will give you their centre lines. Mark these on your photocopy. Where the lines intersect will be your centre point. Now decide which fabric you wish to use. Bear in mind that if your chosen design is too big on 14-count Aida fabric, it will probably fit the space if stitched on a higher count. The rose in the trinket box was stitched on 18-count Aida. A little time spent on these calculations at this stage is well worth the effort to avoid mistakes.

Insert the stitched piece into the door finger plate, trinket box, or hairbrush back, following the manufacturer's instructions.

▶ GLASGOW ROSES	DMC	ANCHOR	MADEIRA
• White	01	02	2402
∷ Gold	832	907	2202
| Light gold	834	874	2510
■ Dark brown	838	380	2005
S Medium plum	3042	870	0807
● Dark green	3362	263	2603
↖ Medium green	3363	262	1602
╲ Light green	3364	260	1603
⊞ Dark pink	3687	68	0604
♡ Medium pink	3688	66	0605
↑ Light pink	3689	49	0607
T Dark plum	3740	873	2614
╱ Light plum	3743	869	2611
∙∙ Magenta	3803	972	2609

Note: Backstitch outlines in dark brown.

Stylized Topiary & Flowers

The classical shapes of topiary trees and stylized flowers were a recurring theme in the Art Nouveau period. These designs are especially appropriate to stitch as cards or gifts for men.

STYLIZED TOPIARY & FLOWERS

YOU WILL NEED

For the Notebook, with a design area measuring 10cm x 6cm (4in x 2³/₈in):

20cm x 15cm (8in x 6in) of antique cream, 22-count Hardanger fabric
Stranded cotton in the colours listed in the appropriate panel
No.24 tapestry needle
Notebook, with an aperture measuring 14cm x 10cm (5¹/₂in x 4in) (for suppliers, see page 40)
Double-sided tape

For the Coaster, with a design area measuring 7cm x 5cm (2³/₄in x 2in):

12.5cm (5in) square of cream, 16-count Aida fabric
Stranded cotton in the colours listed in the appropriate panel
No.26 tapestry needle
Coaster with an aperture measuring 7.5cm (3in) in diameter (for suppliers, see page 40)

For the Trinket Box, with a design area measuring 7.5cm x 5cm (3in x 2in):

15cm (6in) square of sage green, 28-count evenweave fabric
Stranded cotton in the colours listed in the appropriate panel
No26 tapestry needle
Seed beads as listed (optional)
Rosewood trinket box with a circular lid aperture measuring 9cm (3¹/₂in) in diameter (for suppliers, see page 40)

For the Bookmark, with a design area measuring 15cm x 5cm (6in x 2in):

33cm x 20cm (13¹/₄in x 8in) of cream, 28-count evenweave fabric
Stranded cotton in the colours listed in the appropriate panel
No.26 tapestry needle
Matching sewing thread

THE NOTEBOOK

Prepare the fabric and find the centre point as explained on page 4. Using four strands of thread in the needle, cross stitch over two threads of the Hardanger fabric. Alternatively, stitch a simple straight stitch to add texture to the leaves. If using this technique, omit any outlining. If completing in cross stitch, backstitch the outline using two strands of thread in the needle.

Remove the embroidery from the frame and press. Trim the design to 12mm (¹/₂in) from the edge of the notebook opening. Use double-sided tape to secure the design. Fold over the flap at the back of the design and secure with tape.

THE COASTER

Prepare the fabric and find the centre point as explained on page 4. Using two strands of thread in the needle, complete all cross stitching following the chart, and then backstitch outlines with one strand of thread. Assemble the coaster according to the manufacturer's instructions.

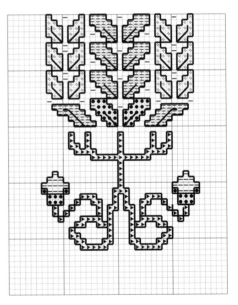

▲ TRINKET BOX TREE		DMC	ANCHOR	MADEIRA
●	Dark green	730	845	1614
ⲷ	Medium green	732	281	1612
⧹	Light green	734	279	1610
▬	Tangerine	742	303	0114
	Dark brown*	838	380	2005
▶	Light brown	3776	1048	2302
	Orange beads	V3.06.720	-	-

Note: Backstitch outlines in dark brown (*backstitch only).*

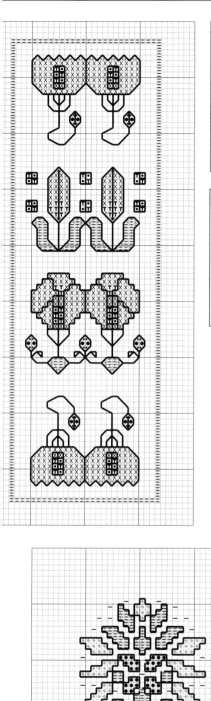

◀ FLOWER BOOKMARK		DMC	ANCHOR	MADEIRA
•	White	01	02	2402
T	Dark plum	315	1019	0810
✕	Plum	316	1017	0809
●	Dark green	730	845	1614
Ⲗ	Medium green	732	281	1612
	Dark brown*	838	380	2005

Note: Backstitch outlines in dark brown (*backstitch only).*

▶ NOTEBOOK TREE		DMC	ANCHOR	MADEIRA
●	Dark green	730	845	1614
Ⲗ	Medium green	732	281	1612
↘	Light green	734	279	1610
▬	Tangerine	742	303	0114
	Dark brown*	838	380	2005
▶	Light brown	3776	1048	2302

Note: Backstitch outlines in dark brown (*backstitch only).*

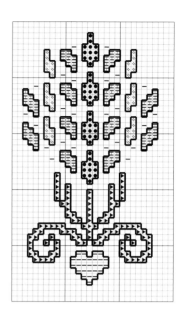

THE TRINKET BOX

Prepare the fabric as explained on page 4. Using two strands of thread and stitching over two threads of the fabric, complete the cross stitching. Then backstitch outlines with one strand of thread. To add texture, substitute orange beads for the tangerine cross stitches (see page 7). To stop the fabric from fraying apply iron-on interfacing to the wrong side of the design. Trim the fabric and assemble the box lid according to the manufacturer's instructions.

THE BOOKMARK

Prepare the fabric as explained on page 4. Using two strands of thread, complete the cross stitching. Backstitch outlines using one strand of thread. Trim the fabric to 2.5cm (1in) from the top and bottom. Fray the fabric down to the stitches. Measure 5cm (2in) in from the side borders and trim. Fold the fabric under, leaving 3mm (1/8in) at each side of the design, and press. Place one flap over the other at the back, turn under the narrow allowance along one edge, and hem the length of the bookmark.

◀ COASTER TREE		DMC	ANCHOR	MADEIRA
●	Dark green	730	845	1614
Ⲗ	Medium green	732	281	1612
↘	Light green	734	279	1610
▬	Tangerine	742	303	0114
	Dark brown*	838	380	2005
▶	Light brown	3776	1048	2302

Note: Backstitch outlines in dark brown (*backstitch only).*

Peacock Needlework Box

Their magnificent tail feathers and iridescent colours made peacocks a natural subject for Art Nouveau. Shiny threads and beads combine to recreate this elegant design.

PEACOCK NEEDLEWORK BOX

YOU WILL NEED

For the Needlework Box, with a design area measuring 21cm x 17.5cm (8³⁄₈in x 7in):

*38cm x 33cm (15in x 13in) of apricot,
28-count evenweave fabric
Stranded embroidery cotton and specialist thread in
the colours listed in the panel
No.26 tapestry needle
Seed beads in the colour listed in the panel*

●

THE EMBROIDERY

Prepare the fabric and find the centre point as explained on page 4. Some areas of the design require stranded cotton and rayon blending filament to be blended. Using two strands of cotton and one of blending filament, follow the instructions on page 7 for working with specialist threads. Work over two threads of the fabric and complete all the cross stitching following the chart. Backstitch the outlines as stated on the thread key. Finally, attach beads where shown by the symbols, following the instructions on page 7.

FINISHING

Remove the embroidery from the frame and wash, if necessary, taking care with the beads. Lightly press the embroidery on the wrong side (avoid using steam as this can affect metallic threads). Assemble the box lid according to the manufacturer's instructions. Alternatively, this piece would be equally suitable framed as a picture.

▶ PEACOCK	DMC	ANCHOR	MADEIRA	MARLITT/ KREINIK
♥ Dark purple x 1 plus purple rayon x 1	550	101	0714	819
◇ Medium purple x 1 plus light purple rayon x 1	552	99	0715	858
O Turquoise	597	168	1110	-
∴ Gold	783	307	2211	-
● Dark brown	838	380	2005	-
I Dark orange	918	341	0314	-
▼ Orange	922	1003	0310	-
↘ Terracotta	975	355	2303	-
Ħ Dark green x 1 plus turquoise rayon x 1	991	189	1204	1053
∷ Olive	3011	845	1607	-
♡ Light olive	3013	842	1605	-
S Dark turquoise x 1 plus purple rayon x 1	3808	170	2508	819
▬ Dark turquoise	3808	170	2508	-
✕ Medium turquoise	3809	169	2507	-
— Aqua x 1 plus dark turquoise rayon x 1	3814	187	1203	1056
Aquamarine (Kreinik)*	-	-	-	Kreinik No.8 Braid
Magenta (Kreinik)*	-	-	-	Kreinik No.8 Braid 242 HL
▣ Deep blue beads	V3.04.930	-	-	-

Note: Backstitch outer edges of large 'eyes' in tail feathers, feather quills on head, and those attaching large 'eye' feathers to tail with Kreinik Aquamarine*. Backstitch purple and turquoise centres of large 'eyes' (referring to photograph if necessary) with Kreinik Magenta* (*used for backstitch only).

ACKNOWLEDGEMENTS

Love and thanks go to my husband Adrian for all his help. The projects were beautifully stitched by Varina Parnell, Daphne White and Jennifer Williams, and framed by Pat Henson of The Crafty Stitcher, Downend, Bristol. I also wish to thank DMC Creative World, Coats Paton Crafts, Framecraft Miniatures Ltd and Fabric Flair for generously supplying the materials for this book.

SUPPLIERS

Stranded cottons, fabrics, beads and needlework box (p36) and Zeigart Appliqué (p14) were supplied by DMC. The finger plate, silver dressing table set and trinket box (p28), notebook, rosewood bowl (p32), spectacles case and porcelain trinket box (p20) were supplied by Framecraft Miniatures Ltd. Marlitt and Kreinik threads were supplied by Coats Paton Crafts and the apricot evenweave (p38) by Fabric Flair Ltd.

Fabric Flair Limited
Northlands Industrial
Estate
Copheap Lane
Warminster
Wiltshire BA12 0BG
Telephone: 01985 846845

FRAMECRAFT
Framecraft Miniatures Ltd
372-376 Summer Lane
Hockley
Birmingham
B19 3QA
Telephone : 0121 212 0551

Addresses for Framecraft stockists worldwide

Ireland Needlecraft Pty Ltd
PO Box 1175
Narre Warren M.D.C.
Victoria 3805
Australia

Danish Art Needlework
PO Box 442,
Lethbridge
Alberta T1J 3Z1
Canada

Sanyei Imports
PO Box 5,
Hashima Shi
Gifu 501-62
Japan

The Embroidery Shop
286 Queen Street
Masterton
New Zealand

Anne Brinkley Designs Inc.
246 Walnut Street
Newton
Mass. 02160,
USA

S A Threads and
Cottons Ltd
43 Somerset Road
Cape Town
South Africa

For more information on your nearest stockist of embroidery cotton, contact the following:

DMC
(also distributors of Zweigart fabrics)

UK
DMC Creative World Ltd
62 Pullman Road,
Wigston
Leicester LE8 2DY
Telephone: 0116 2811040

USA
The DMC Corporation
Port Kearney, Building 10
South Kearney
N.J. 07032
Telephone: 201 589 0606

AUSTRALIA
DMC (Australia) Pty Ltd
PO Box 317
Earlwood
NSW 2206
Telephone: 02 9559 3088

COATS AND ANCHOR
UK
Coats Paton Crafts
McMullen Road
Darlington
Co. Durham DL1 1YQ
Telephone: 01325 381010

USA
Coats & Clark
PO Box 24998
Dept COI
Greenville SC 29616
Telephone: 800 243 0810

AUSTRALIA
Coats Spencer Crafts
Private Bag 15
Mulgrave North
Victoria 3181
Telephone: 03 9561 2288

MADEIRA
UK
Madeira Threads (UK) Ltd
Thirsk Industrial Park
York Road
Thirsk
North Yorkshire YO7 3BX
Telephone: 01845 524880

USA
Madeira Marketing Ltd
600 East 9th Street
Michigan City
IN 46360
Telephone: 219 873 1000

AUSTRALIA
Penguin Threads Pty Ltd
25-27 Izett Street
Prahran
Victoria 3181
Telephone: 03 9529 4400